D1327038

GARDENS ILLUSTRATED

KNOW HOW

PLANTING

PUTTING DOWN ROOTS

by

PENELOPE
HOBHOUSE

JOHN BROWN PUBLISHING

FOREWORD

Most gardening techniques are very simple and can be discovered by using common sense and imagination. Getting the soil right is the first priority. Good, well-prepared tilth with plenty of earthworms is obviously going to give plants a good start. If the worms are happy plants will probably thrive. Planting correctly is another essential. This includes choosing plants with well-developed root systems, and avoiding those which have been badly grown or are pot-bound. Each plant or group of plants must have the right soil and climatic conditions. It is no use planting acid-loving plants in alkaline soil or planting the moisture lovers where they will dry out.

Established woody plants need pruning and training, often on an annual basis, and most soft-stemmed perennials need dividing in order to maintain their vigour. The most fun in gardening comes from making new plants from old; propagating from cuttings and growing newplants or replacements from seed.

Gardening carefully and thoughtfully brings its own rewards. The pleasure of watching things grow, waiting patiently, not hurrying results, that is the best way to gain experience. Like the garden itself, gardening know-how grows with time.

Penelope Hobhouse

Mary Hill

The old adage 'a penny for the plant and a pound for the planting' is still a good guide. In other words, take trouble, and take equal care with everything from large trees to homely annuals. Every plant deserves to be given an environment in which it will thrive, with a suitable aspect and appropriate soil, but it also needs special care during its introduction to new conditions. During the transition between being reared and getting established in its garden role, whether container-grown, or with bare roots, a plant is especially vulnerable to neglect. This continues both in the period immediately after planting and while it is still immature.

A plant must be in good condition before planting. Most plants today come in plastic containers, where the compost is held together by hair-like fibrous roots that should continue feeding and growing until planting time and after. These mat-like roots should only half fill the pot before the plant is ready to plant. This means that they should establish easily when planted.

The condition of the plant is not the only thing. Preparation of suitable soil with adequate drainage is even more important. Follow guidance on the type of soil required for a plant and ensure your garden soil is in as good as condition possible before planting. The book on soil in this series will provide a good general introduction to soil management.

All plants dislike root disturbance and will cease growing for a period after being put in the ground until their fibrous roots have started re-absorbing nourishment from the surrounding soil. If appropriately chosen for soil and climate, they should settle in quickly to their new environment. Ideally no plant should be put under stress by planting in extreme temperatures but of course it is possible to plant container-grown stock at almost any time of year unless the ground is frozen too hard to dig. If planting in a dry period remember to water adequately in the following weeks.

CHOOSING PLANTS

I like to buy plants well ahead of planting so that an essential 'potting-on' process can be carried out. When obtaining plants, whether trees, shrubs, perennials or annuals, do not buy those that are pot-bound, with roots showing through the base of the pot. When the plant is tapped out - usually by giving a hard rap on its base - the roots should be visible but not curled round and constricted. If a large tap root has grown out of the base of the container cut this off before planting but only use the plant if there are plenty of fibrous growing roots actually inside the pot. If , when tapped out, the compost falls apart exposing the roots it is not ready for planting; it has not had sufficient time in the container to get established, with its thread-like roots - the feeding roots -

PLANTS WHICH HAVE been allowed to become root-bound should be repotted and given time to establish new fibrous roots in new compost before planting out. If a main root is twisted round, uncurl it, trim it and scratch out fibrous roots to ensure they spread into new compost.

11

THE PERFECT ROOT BALL can be seen when the plant has made a network of fibrous roots, sufficient to hold the compost together when the plant is tipped out of its pot. Then it is ready for planting out. If, however, the compost falls off when the pot is tipped, quickly replant in the original pot and then wait until the plant is better established before planting out. The delay in planting is worth the trouble since the plant will establish in the soil more successfully.

able to make a sufficient mat to hold the planting medium together. This sort of situation can arise when buying plants that have only been potted up a short time. Repot immediately and wait a few weeks for the fibrous roots to establish.

POTTING ON

Plants grown in a soil-based medium, given a chance to develop a sturdy root system before planting, adapt much more quickly to their new situation. Many nurseries still make their own soil-based mixtures for their containerised plants, and these plants will take less time to establish in the new environment. However when buying from a garden centre you may find the plant has been grown in a loamless compost (a mixture of peat, sand and perlite -

much easier to manage in large-scale production). You can tell if this is so if the plant and pot are very light. It is advisable to pot on into the next size of container using a soil-based potting medium. Do not make it too large or the plant could become water-logged. The medium can be home-made from a mixture of one-third sand, one-third garden loam and one-third peat or peat substitute, plus some slow-release fertiliser. I like to add grit in the base of each pot to ensure good drainage. The actual planting can be delayed until the fibrous roots have 'filled' the new container and may take a few weeks.

Most plants need at least a month or six weeks in a container after potting before planting out in their permanent home. A reliable nursery may let you have the plants but will tell you to wait before

WHEN REPOTTING as part of the potting-on process, tap out the plant and place it in a larger container with a new soil-based potting medium under the base and tucked in around the edge of the pot. Do not move to a pot too much bigger than the original one as the plant may well get over-watered if in too large a container. A potting medium can be home-made using a mixture of one-third sand, one-third garden loam and one-third peat or a peat substitute, plus some slow-release fertiliser and a little grit in the base.

17

planting, giving the plants a few more weeks to fill the pot. Some plants such as roses take a particularly long time to get established in a container, making new fibrous roots very slowly. Roses are best planted bare-root in winter or before their leaves have unfurled in spring or they need a few months in a container to ensure they have made enough fibrous root to survive the shock of being planted out to their permanent site.

A plant continues to grow while still in its pot but at planting time has to push its fibrous roots out into the surrounding soil in order to receive nourishment and continue to grow. If the plant has been well grown to the right size for the container and the soil is of suitable texture and has been well prepared, establishment should be easy. Good nurseries will regularly transplant and re-pot their young stock to help keep the roots compact, and thus minimise checks in growth at planting time.

PLANTING OUT

The existing condition of the soil and site will affect the ease of planting. Individual trees, shrubs and perennials need holes large enough to allow loose soil to be packed around the root-ball to stimulate the fibrous roots. Ideally, the hole could be almost twice the size of the container or root-ball. The more compacted the soil, the larger the hole should be. If planting bare root plants, particularly if moving a plant in your own garden, the holes should be wide and deep enough for the main roots to be spread out, although some longer roots can be trimmed.

GROWING PLANTS IN CONTAINERS, rather than planting them out in the soil, can be the best way to provide certain plants with the right conditions for growth. This is because some plants, including agapanthus, love to grow very tightly packed in their pots. They will flower more abundantly each successive year, especially if they are fed immediately after flowering and before the leaves have died down.

If you are planting large trees or shrubs, break up the hard pan found under the topsoil. Unless the area is really compacted, I find it better to fill in with whatever soil is around, rather than using a specially prepared mix; you can find you have created a water sump that can drown the plant if it doesn't drain away, and the water may freeze in cold

MAKE YOUR PLANTING HOLE in the flower bed twice as wide and deeper than the container in which the plant has been sitting. Dig the hole before removing the plant fully from its pot, after checking the root ball is ready. Preparing a decent hole is as important as getting the soil right. This is especially important when planting in heavy clay.

23

weather. These days, when large trees are moved and replanted by specialist tree firms, very little soil amendment is advised because some tree roots, if at first given a pampered root run, will refuse to venture out into less accommodating soil beyond. It is also best to stake only large, unstable specimens and even then place the stake - or double stake attached with a cross bar - as low as possible on the trunk. Contractors can use invisible staking with strong posts fixed around the root ball underground. Most woody plants benefit from being left to develop their own root system that will resist prevailing winds. Tight staking does not encourage this.

The final soil level around the stems of herbaceous plants or the trunk of a tree should match the original level in the pot, but there are exceptions like clematis, which benefits from deeper planting, and peonies, which don't like to be buried too deep. Rhizomes of irises and corms of cyclamen need to be near the surface.

If you find the roots of a new container-grown plant are coiled in a ball, they should be gently teased out while trying to keep as much compost around them as possible. I 'scratch' the sides of the compost to encourage the fibrous roots to escape and spread. You can do this quite fiercely. Make certain after planting that the soil covers the top of the potting compost, which, especially if mainly peat-based, can dry out very quickly, and is very difficult to re-saturate.

Before planting a perennial scheme and/or annuals, I like to 'place' all the pots on the soil, arrang-

through the seasons. Plants, particularly woody ones, are often planted too close together to get some sort of instant effect. This is a reasonable and practical approach but the plants will need thinning later. One solution is to deliberately over-plant initially but select a proportion of specimens which are not long lived to place between the more permanent plants. Tree lupins, *Euphorbia characais* and its subspecies, cistus, hebes, lavenders, rosemary and santolina are either short-lived or getting woddy and unsightly within a short period and can be taken out of a scheme after a few years. Biennials such as *Reseda luteola*, *Eryngium giganteum* (Miss Willmott's Ghost), sweet rocket (*Hesperis matrionalis*), most verbascums (some are true perennials), *Isatis tinctoria* (woad) and *Salvia sclarea*

'Turkestanica' are good temporary fillers for a sunny area, and foxgloves and forget-me-nots will thrive in light shade. Annuals can, of course, also be used between shrubs and perennials to give impact until the other plants mature.

I soak all pots or bare roots before planting, and water frequently during the next weeks. Thick mulch, using organic matter such as compost, leaf mould or gravel, added around the base of the plant will help preserve moisture and prevent weed germination. Mulch should not, however, be put over the crowns of herbaceous plants or packed too tightly around a woody stem.

STAKE A YOUNG TREE if it is necessary. Make sure the stake is as short as possible to allow some movement and encourage the shrub or tree to establish its own strong and stabilising root system. Lining the stem will prevent damaging the stem and allow a little room for growth. Use adjustable ties when staking any tree or shrub because it is important to remember to loosen the ties as the width of the trunk or stem increases.

PLANTING SHRUBS

Most shrubs are best planted or transplanted in the autumn or early winter while the ground is still warm, but deciduous trees and shrubs can be planted in any good weather during the winter. Evergreen shrubs that lose moisture through their leaves, should be planted in September or April. Alternatively they can be dug up with a large root ball and containerised until a convenient planting time, probably in spring. Often the larger evergreen trees or shrubs are balled and burlapped, rather than potted. This involves wrapping the root ball tightly in hessian or burlap. All evergreens dehydrate while roots are re-establishing in their new home. The same common sense rules apply to moving evergreens in the garden, always make sure to keep as much soil as possible attached to the roots. Evergreen shrubs and trees, exposed to drying winds or sun, should have their foliage sprayed regularly to prevent dehydration.

Roses and some field-grown deciduous trees and shrubs, which develop few fibrous roots in containers, are best planted in the autumn with bare roots, as soon as possible after they have been dug from their nursery site.

HERBACEOUS PLANTS

Herbaceous plants should be planted or transplanted in early autumn or spring. I prefer to plant bare rootstock in autumn and containerised plants in spring. A hole large enough to take the containerised plant can easily become a water sump if there is a wet

winter, and more plants are lost by having their roots freeze or drown in water than from lack of hardiness. Early autumn is the ideal time to reshuffle your borders, but, as you work, keep any bare roots covered to protect them against drying winds.

I re-pot new plants obtained from a nursery in my own compost mix and keep them in an unheated cold frame, watered very sparingly through the winter, planting out in early April.

HARDY HERBACEOUS plants can be put in their permanent sites in autumn or spring. More tender types are best planted out in April or May as the soil begins to warm up.

Supports for tall, soft stemmed herbaceous plants can be added in early summer when the plants have reached about a third of their ultimate height - they disappear as the foliage grows.

There are always occasions when you are offered a desirable perennial in full leaf and flower growing in a friend's garden or when your own scheme need changes in the middle of the summer. Whatever the season it is usually possible to move it safely, although it may not perform again until the following

HAZEL TWIGS are an attractive alternative to bamboo and string for staking perennials. Most should be staked in May and twigs should be about two-thirds the plant's final size.

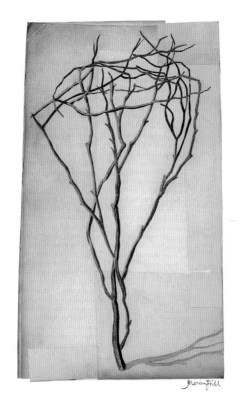

year. Cut away much of the top growth (especially the flowers which by going to seed use up extra plant energy), keep it shaded and puddle it in, providing regular watering after care.

PLANTING ANNUALS

The smaller the plant, the more vulnerable it is to drought and weed competition. Before setting out annuals or plants such as tender shrubs grown as annuals, it is best to fork over the planting area, incorporating some organic material. Make sure the home-grown or bought-in plants are hardened off and the threat of frost has passed. Hold the pots in a tank of water until all the air from the compost is expelled and the bubbles stop. If planting a large area it can be convenient and timesaving to fill a wheelbarrow with water in which a batch of plants can sit while they absorb the moisture. Having prepared the hole, add a handful of organic fertiliser around the root of each plant, before gently firming it in place. On heavy clay, especially if it is inclined to be water-logged, it is advisable to put gravel in the bottom of each hole. Annuals will take a few weeks to establish, so it is best to water regularly. When planting is complete dress the remaining bare soil with a moisture-retaining and weed-suppressing mulch. Most annuals, once they produce new growth, can manage without further cosseting.

MOVING ESTABLISHED PLANTS

I move plants around my garden all the time. Some areas simply get overcrowded. Every planting scheme is 'edited' at least once a year. Some plants get overrun by others and 'thugs' begin to get the upper hand. They will not only damage weaker plants but will spoil the carefully planned garden picture, in which relative sizes and proportions are a vital element. Most areas in a garden need periodic reshuffling and plants, especially perennials, need lifting and dividing in order to make them per-

WHEN MOVING established plants, dig up the roots with a spade or fork keeping as much soil as possible attached to the roots. Place a on a mat or plastic sheet to move.

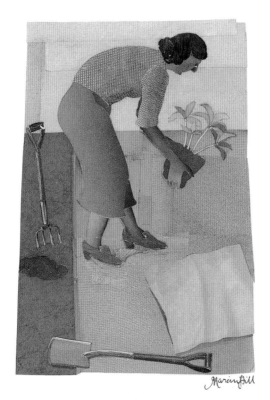

form better. Many perennials need dividing every three or four years or they will cease to flower well; others, such as peonies, hate disturbance and flower better and better as they mature on site.

Shrubs may out-grow their original position and have to be transferred to a new place in the garden or simply removed if severe pruning is not suitable. I have a beautiful specimen viburnum, *Vibernum x hillieri* 'Winton', in my walled garden which sends out horizontal branches. It is growing too large for its site, spreading over a neighbouring path. Impossible to trim back without spoiling its elegant shape, I will have to find a new position for it.

Sometimes plants are moved because they are not thriving; it is easy to recognise the symptoms of stress: poor performance, unhealthy leaves and lack of growth. This will be because they are not happy in the conditions and soil provided. The aspect may have altered; an area open and sunny at planting time may now be shaded by neighbouring plants.

Plants, both woody and perennial, are best moved or divided in autumn or early spring. Sick plants can be potted up and nursed through a period of recovery and planted again in a more appropriate situation. When moving an evergreen shrub make sure you dig it with a good root ball and plant again as soon as possible, if necessary cutting back some of the top growth so that it has fewer leaves to transpire. A spray can prevent excessive transpiration. Place the root ball in a plastic or hessian sheet and wrap it tightly as you move it. Water well before digging up and prepare a hole larger than the root ball

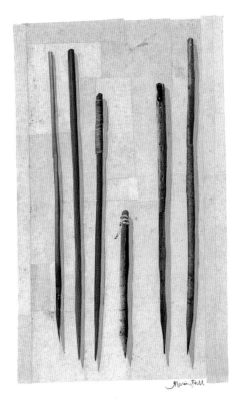

45

ACKNOWLEDGEMENTS

ILLUSTRATIONS by Marian Hill
DESIGNED by Roger Walton
PRODUCTION by Imago Publishing Ltd

Photograph of Penelope Hobhouse by Charles Hopkinson

First published in Great Britain by John Brown Publishing Ltd,
The New Boathouse, 136-142 Bramley Road, London
W10 6SR

ISBN 1-902212-277

Printed and bound in China for Imago

GARDENS

ILLUSTRATED

Take out a SPECIAL OFFER subscription to the world's leading gardening magazine. Only £29.50 for 10 issues, a saving of 15%.

I would like to take out a subscription to GARDENS ILLUSTRATED

☐ 1 year (10 issues): £29.50 UK; £45.00 Europe, £60.00 rest of world

☐ 2 years (20 issues): £58.00 UK; £89.00 Europe, £110.00 rest of world

☐ I enclose a cheque payable to John Brown Publishing (sterling cheques only)

for £ _____

I would like to pay by credit/debit card. Please charge my:

☐ VISA ☐ MASTERCARD ☐ AMEX ☐ EUROCARD

☐ CONNECT ☐ SWITCH: issue no./start date [_____]

Card Number ☐☐☐☐ ☐☐☐☐ ☐☐☐☐ ☐☐☐☐

Expiry Date ☐☐☐☐

Signature   Date
_____

Name
_____

Address
_____
                                        Postcode
_____

Telephone   Email
_____

Send this form to: GARDENS ILLUSTRATED, SUBSCRIPTIONS, FREEPOST (SWB837), BRISTOL BS32 0ZZ   (No stamp needed in the UK). Or phone 01454 618 905.

Money back guarantee: you may cancel your subscription at any time if not completely satisfied and receive a refund on all unmailed issues. GARDENS ILLUSTRATED is published by John Brown Publishing Ltd, The New Boathouse,136-142 Bramley Road, London W10 6SR